The Year
in Sweden

© Bokförlaget Max Ström 2009
© Photo: Each respective photographer
Text: Kim Loughran
Editor: Kevin Billinghurst
Design: Patric Leo
Layout: Petra Ahston Inkapööl
Repro: Elanders Fälth & Hässler, Sweden
Printing: Livonia Print, Latvia, 2016
www.maxstrom.se
Tenth impression
ISBN: 978-91-7126-165-6

The Year in Sweden

KIM LOUGHRAN

BOKFÖRLAGET MAX STRÖM

IT'S ROUGHLY THE shape and size of California. But with 9 million people, just a quarter of the Golden State's population. Fewer movie stars but more seasons. There are three traditional regions: on top is Norrland, with vast forests and ore deposits; Svealand, with tens of thousands of lakes, is in the middle; and in the south is Götaland, with its stony highlands and rich plains.

The Swedish population is largely homogeneous, but there are five linguistic minorities and more immigrants than you might expect — 15 percent of the population have at least one parent born abroad. Sweden is one of the world's wealthiest countries and among the most contented. Longevity is high: 83 years for women, 79 for men. Sweden is a constitutional monarchy and member of the European Union, although without abandoning the krona for the euro.

It is a patient place. You silently endure until the daylight returns after its winter hibernation. You wait in line without complaint. Check-out assistants are relaxed and unhurried. Friends listen attentively to you — and if you are patient, you will make many.

Natural beauty is never far away, even when you're dead — this country has countless scenic cemeteries. Swedes are self-effacing, helpful, pragmatic. Like the Japanese, good inventors and good copiers. History lists iron-fisted monarchs, drunken poets, enigmatic movies, beautiful sports and that cheeky little Pippi Longstocking. Cleverness sustains Sweden through bad times. Tolerance is easing it into the new century.

Swedes live and love and tackle bus queues respectfully. Some see placidness; I see a template for urban interplay in the new century, city people aware of Nature. And every week in summer I still spot the most beautiful girl I've ever seen in my life. That happens when you love a country a lot.

Here are twelve snapshots.

Kim Loughran
PS. That whole ÅÄÖ business? Let me get back to you.

Stockholm seen from the freshwater side. North of the Old Town with the massive rectangle of the Royal Palace is the Baltic Sea, its waters only slightly saline. In the foreground, City Hall and its tapered brick tower.

(Overleaf) Speeding over finger-thin ice, a chill bath just a stumble away, tour skaters rejoice in cold, clear winter days. By listening to the ice "sing" as they glide over it, experienced skaters can judge the strength of the surface ahead.

JAN

WELCOME TO WEEK 1. Every week in the Swedish calendar has a number. This combines efficiency and inefficiency: instead of scheduling a meeting for a day of "the week that begins with the 5th", you suggest Week 32. Easy to find in a diary, impossible to remember without one. Only Week 1 and Week 52 are easy to keep track of.

Wherever you are, it's cold. The trees are bare, and you can now see from one side of a city park to the other. Even in the extreme south, the mean temperature is zero Celsius, although the country's western face to the North Atlantic and the Gulf Stream provides a relatively mild winter climate considering Stockholm's shared latitude with, for example, Anchorage, Alaska.

The last of the Christmas holidays is the thirteenth day after Christmas, celebrating the visit of the Three Magi to the infant Jesus. The following Monday, schoolchildren slip back to their desks after the holidays — still missing are those taking unapproved time on distant charter islands. July has always been the major holiday period because of the weather; now there's competition from December-January — also because of the weather. Charter flights to Spain started in 1955, flashbulbs popping for the first departures.

These days, Thailand is the most popular destination. Nine million people generate ten million charter trips annually. One poll said that 60 percent would prefer more vacation time to a bigger paycheck. Sweden's travel operators are efficient. When the 2004 tsunami hit southeast Asia, 4,500 Swedes were in Thailand. The effective help provided by Sweden's biggest Thailand operator, Fritidsresor, has since been included in Harvard University's leadership training curriculum.

This is the poorest sales month for Systembolaget, the state alcohol retail monopoly. By their philosophy, poorest is also best. The monopoly grew from an 18th-century decree banning the use of grain for private distilling — poor harvests had led to a scarcity of bread, a major food. The monopoly is cursed, ridiculed — and

The spires of the capital spy on winter strollers on Lake Mälaren. The taller one is Riddarholmskyrkan, one of Stockholm's oldest buildings. The steeple to the right belongs to the German Church. At one time, German was the language most used in the Old Town.

From the jetties in Gothenburg, sailing ships once freighted timber and wheat to England. This port was the last view of the old country for hundreds of thousands of Swedes who left for new lives in America in the 19th and early 20th centuries. Ferries now carry passengers north to Norway, west to Denmark and south to Germany.

beneficial. Juggling with taxes and tariffs while fighting off EU trade infringement charges has produced results. Swedish alcohol consumption, once among Europe's highest, dropped to among the lowest after the monopoly became law. Alcoholism is seen as either an illness or a rebellion against conformity.

The state has also produced booze. Before it was sold to a French company in 2008, Absolut Vodka was earning zillions for the same state that took every opportunity to rap its population on the knuckles for its drinking habits. But the message about the dangers of drink was a mixed one, and the state no longer manufactures demon rum while tut-tutting its users. Systembolaget is an efficient monopoly: the selection of beers, wines and spirits is broad, sophisticated and available anywhere. If you live in the countryside far from a System outlet, they'll send your order by post to the nearest food store.

Coffee al fresco in January? Swedes drink more java per capita than anyone in the world after the Finns. And in the depth of winter — at least in the southern third of the country — mocca addicts who are also smokers take their espressi outdoors under radiator heaters.

Culture blossoms in deepest winter. Myriad courses in art, language, music, cooking, dress-making, understanding your pony. And people buying theatre seats and popcorn. The Swedish word for cinema is bio, derived from the Biograph, an early German projector. The Guldbagge Awards for film (the word translates to Gold Bug, but the actual prize is a 1.2-kilo copper beetle) are awarded with fanfare in January. Swedes are avid moviegoers — apparently everyone goes one and a half times a year. Some swear that watching subtitled movies from childhood helps foreign language skills, a possible explanation for the Swedes' excellent English compared to most people from Germany, France or Spain, where markets are big enough to support dubbing. Sweden and Denmark top EU rankings for state support of culture and numbers of citizens putting rear ends on seats.

At the end of the month, the architectural gem that is Stockholm's Liljevalchs museum gallery opens its salon for amateur artists. The salon is open to all comers, but almost a century ago it was the major entry point to the art establishment. Easily the most successful Swedish artist is Carl Larsson (1853–1919). He has visibly impacted Swedish taste and might be considered the aesthetic root of IKEA. He painted countless interiors with loving precision, a diary of life in a perfect home. His wife Karin, a designer and artist, once commissioned a rocking chair from a local carpenter who delivered the finished product in the gloom of night because its plain lines embarrassed him.

They say it used to rain dead Christmas trees on Knut's name day, twenty days after Christmas when children took a last whirl around the tree before packing down the ornaments. By tradition, the trees would be jettisoned on the nearest pavement. These days, the tarry wood is collected to fire furnaces for district heating.

Fewer dinner invitations this month. Christmas budgets are overdrawn. But after the mad partying of December, Swedes are pining for that insulating darkness again. Thinking time.

One of the delights of winter in northern Sweden is the Aurora Borealis, or northern light. Old beliefs said that the Aurora was a school of heavenly herring or swans frozen in the air. Current science sees only atmospheric molecules ionized by cosmic and solar radiation. Lucky observers will also hear a sound.

(Overleaf) The lighthouse on Öja Island, first erected in 1691, is the oldest in the Stockholm archipelago. Since 1535, Öja has been home to generations of pilots who boarded incoming ships and helped navigate the labyrinth of islands to reach Stockholm. A sea rescue unit is based here. At last count, the Stockholm archipelago included some 24,000 islands.

Åre is one of
Scandinavia's best
ski resorts for
families — in the
February school
holiday, the ski lifts
never stop. It's also
a great party town,
where rock bands
make their names
as live performers.

(Overleaf) One of
the magnificent
rivers of the north,
Österdalälven.
The mighty
northern rivers
have long been
generous providers
of hydropower
although 50 percent
of Sweden's
electricity now
comes from
nuclear plants.

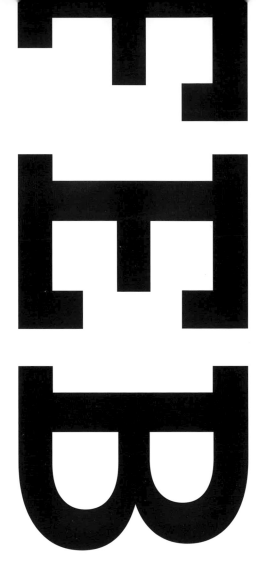

IF NOVEMBER IS the month when the fewest children are born, that would make February the least erotic month. Urban legend has it that most Swedish babies are born nine months to the day after the feelgood festival of Midsummer Eve, when cavorting is on everyone's mind. But February can be cold and gloomy and if sex represents comfort as well as fun, surely now would be a perfect time?

How sex-fixated are Swedes? Most of them will tell you: *lagom*. It means 'sufficiently' and the word carries a connotation of good judgment. The New York Times has said that the roots of sexual liberation in Scandinavia are the state-sponsored social movements for women's rights, sex education and health care, plus freedom of expression. Various forms of feminism have been an ingrained part of Swedish culture since Viking times. The modern incarnation is less concerned with sexuality than boosting healthy families.

For those too young to agonise over sex, February brings sports week, a break from school and a last chance to go skiing. The vacation period is staggered so the popular ski resorts are not gridlocked. At this stage of the winter, daylight is coming back and temperatures are milder than just a month ago, although there's still plenty of snow.

Awaiting the short growing season, shoppers are still dependent on produce from hothouses in Holland and Spain or freeze-shipped from Thailand, Kenya or Brazil. But home-grown vegies are never forgotten and a seasonal favourite is mashed turnips and boiled pork sausage with lashings of mustard. This is a foodie nation, with more cookbooks published per capita than in any other country.

It's cold enough now to quieten even the Lebanese and Syrian sellers at outdoor market stalls. In other weather, Stockholm's fruit and vegetable markets are cacophonous with shouted bargains and claims of the sweetest oranges. The spikes for Swedish immigration in the last half-century began with an influx of Hungarians following the 1956 uprising, then the exodus of Jews from Poland in 1968, the

A farm on the southern plains. Sweden's society evolved from farmsteads rather than villages. The transformation from rural to urban life in the 19th and 20th centuries was relatively abrupt. Many major roads cut right through old farms.

The west coast island of Tjörn (facing page), once home to a thriving fishing fleet, now a beloved summer retreat for Gothenburgians and other lucky souls. The 'Madeira of the North' is on the edge of the Kattegat, the mostly shallow sea that links the North Sea with the Baltic.

The bizarre ice hotel near Jukkasjärvi, in the far north, rebuilt every year in a new version. In November, snow sprayed onto steel forms freezes, and architects and artists shape ice blocks for the first guests in December. The hotel thaws every April.

(Overleaf) Enchanting — and bitterly cold. The temperature was -33° C in the little town of Byske on the north-central coast when the picture was taken.

flight of opposition sympathisers from Chile after Pinochet took power in 1973, the Iran-Iraq war of 1980–88, the confusion and carnage in the Horn of Africa in the 1990s and the invasion of Iraq from 2003. Just under half of all asylum requests are granted. More than 13 percent of the country's inhabitants were born abroad and the influx is making the country more youthful demographically.

Enter the snowdrop (*Galántus niválís*). What a guy! A graceful white head drooping pensively on a slender neck, battling up through the snow. The six-petalled snowdrop ignores cold, obeying only the primeval call of light.

The interminable
mud of March.
Spring inches
northward at a
snail's pace. Unlike
some countries,
Sweden's spring
has no fixed date
but is determined
region by region,
defined as the
first week of
temperatures over
zero. Or when birch
leaves reach the
size of mouse ears.

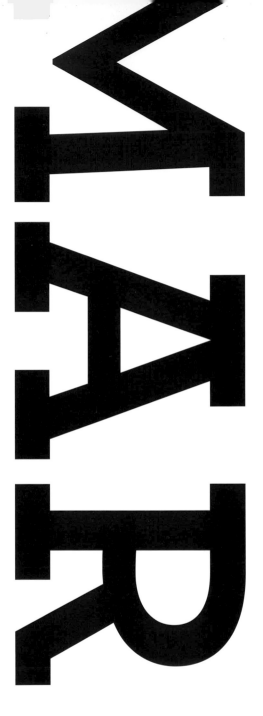

A TRANSITION MONTH, LONG on slush. Step outside in fine shoes at your own risk. But day and night hours will return to equilibrium about the 20th, and winter's agonies are forgotten at the first sighting of yellow coltsfoot in a roadside ditch. By the end of the month, the crocus appears in the south. Crocuses don't grow wild but almost every garden has them. Sweden is poorly suited to gardening because of the temperature swings and short growing season, but everyone with a patch of land tries. Almost a hundred years ago, cities set aside plots for factory-working families to plant flowers and watch real grass grow. Huts on the allotments are legally limited in size to prevent their use as dwellings.

Bears are in their last month of hibernation (no, there are no polar bears in Sweden) but deer can occasionally be seen in city suburbs, nibbling at early tulip bulbs.

Long-distance or tour skaters are still plying the archipelagos, where virgin ice too thin to stand on will support you if you're moving fast enough. Skaters say the ice will sing its thickness, warning you of danger, but it's still safer earlier in the winter when the ice is sturdier. The hardest part must be the test dip: skaters' clubs sometimes ask prospective members to jump into freezing water so they can practise getting out. Skaters carry a pair of ice prods on a string around their necks, handy for gripping the ice in case of a dunk; dry clothes in plastic bags can also serve as flotation devices. Once in the water, you've got 20 minutes at most. Ice-skating originated in Scandinavia about a thousand years ago, when some unnamed genius came up with the idea of tying polished bone to footwear.

Outdoor exercise, particularly in winter, underpins the population's good health. The global battle between the couch and the great outdoors is being fought here too, although the toughening effect of a winter climate serves Sweden well. Almost everyone has at least stood on skis by the time they reach adulthood.

The return of the sun brings immediate warmth and a piercing brightness. Take along a foam rubber cushion and you can stop and relax on your walk. Stockholmers flock to the paths along Riddarfjärden Bay at the first hint of blue sky.

The lighthouse at Vinga, an island off the west coast (facing page). The first beacon — a basket hung on a scaffold — was lit here in the early 17th century when battles with the Danes raged over what is now southern Sweden.

One of Sweden's five large carnivores (that's including Man), the bear is a protected species, although limited hunting is allowed to cull the population. When cubs emerge in spring from mother's hibernation, they eat mainly grass and leaves.

(Overleaf) The Great Race. On the first Sunday in March, more than 15,000 cross-country skiers re-enact the historic flight by Gustav Vasa, the leader of a rebel movement against the marauding Danes.

The pinnacle event of the skiing year is not a high-purse race involving slalom brand names but the world's oldest mass ski race, the Vasaloppet, on the first Sunday of March. If there's no snow, they'll manufacture it. More than 15,000 skiers from dozens of countries compete. The race covers the 90 kilometres separating the towns of Sälen and Mora, recalling the 1521 flight of the renegade Gustav Vasa, later king, from Denmark's Kristian. The starting gun brings to life a mobile mosaic of thousands of battling skis and ski poles. Wool-covered heads bow to the snow and shoot like shotgun pellets into the forest. King Carl Gustaf and his son Prince Carl Philip have done the race, presumably both for its iconic thrill and to honour its royal history.

The monarchy enjoys continued popular support. But Swedish monarchs are restricted to opening bridges and parliament, with less power than any other European royal heads of state.

Mountain hiking in April, with the snow still bountiful and the days long. We are in the Sarek National Park, looking southwest. Following America's lead, Sweden was the first European country with designated national parks.

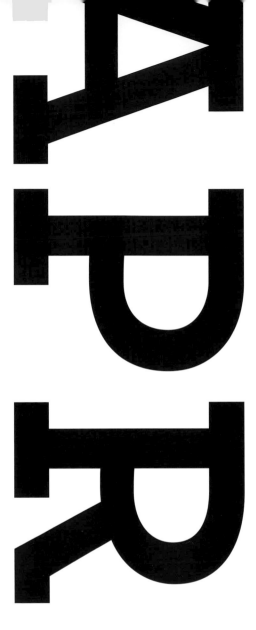

O UTDOOR MARKETS FILL with feather dusters ... wait, those are dyed feathers wired to bunches of birch twigs. You put the twigs in water to light up your home as you watch tiny green leaves emerge to hasten spring. In small towns and suburbs, little girls dress as freckle-faced witches "just in from Blue Mountain". Younger brothers in tow, they knock on doors to shake down their neighbours for candy Easter eggs.

Ice still covers northern lakes, and jigging (fishing through a hole in the ice) can be a pleasure if you're lucky enough to catch a bit of warming sun. But it can be dangerous recreation; taking a chance on the thickness of April ice has led to many an abrupt dip. Those who stay dry might bring home a perch or, in the north, a char.

April 30th is the last day motorists can drive with studded tyres, barring menacing snowstorms. Studs rip up asphalt, spraying dangerous particles into the air. Winter tyres, studded or just deep-treaded, are obligatory from December 1st to March 31st. Everyone taking a driving licence has to learn to handle a car on ice. Scheduling your test for summer months doesn't buy any reprieve; the exam can be done on oil slicks. By default, headlights are on when you start your vehicle because there's no way to legislate for daylight visibility — shifting weather can turn bright sunshine to murkiness in minutes. It's a big gain in safety at zero cost or inconvenience.

Road deaths hover around 400 a year. Postal vehicles drive on the right like everyone else but with the steering wheel on the kerb side so the driver can service mailboxes without having to get out. More than every second person eligible for a driving licence has a car and almost every fourth car on the road is a Volvo.

April could not end more dramatically: bonfires rage across the country in aggressive farewell to winter cold. Walpurgis

Thawed snow fills rivers, creeks and wetlands. The peregrine falcon has found its way back to Sweden from the Mediterranean coasts or North Africa. Cranes are nesting in carefully protected swamps. Urban Swedes get the outdoor urge.

A field of wood anemones! The humble *Anemone nemorosa* grows mainly in the south. It is poisonous but was used in the past as a rheumatism cure. Inspires poetry among romantic youth.

The Rosendal organic gardens and café bring Stockholmers out of their winter shells even before the snow has melted.

(Overleaf) A fiery farewell to winter's torment. A pagan enjoyment that has become one of the most important secular rituals of the Swedish year. In legend, Walpurgis Night was when the witches partied. Now, amateur choirs harmonise and speeches ring out as the flames crackle every April 30th.

Night, the 30th of April, is a breathtakingly pagan rite, with choruses gathering round pyres to dispel the cruel winter and conjure up a good harvest year. Romance in the air and empty bottles in the gutter.

Birds are back. White wagtails can be seen in car-parks foraging for insects. Early arrivals include swans, larks, plovers and doves. Tropical birds wait as long as they can — the willow warbler, for example. Among the last to show up will be the honey buzzard, following the coastline to navigate almost up to the far north.

After centuries of
enmity and frequent
raids back and forth
across the ice, the
Scandinavian sibling
nations of Denmark
and Sweden now
have a physical
link in the Öresund
Bridge. It connects
the Swedish city
of Malmö with the
Danish capital,
Copenhagen,
cross-fertilising
two busy regions to
create Scandinavia's
largest conurbation.
About 50,000
people cross daily.

(Overleaf)
The spring flood
in Gautsträsk, a
protected marshland
area in the far north.
Gautsträsk supports
a rich variety of
bushes and trees,
especially spruce,
the preferred
harvest for forestry
industries. Old
spruce trees are
now relatively rare.
A few traditionally
managed farms still
operate here.

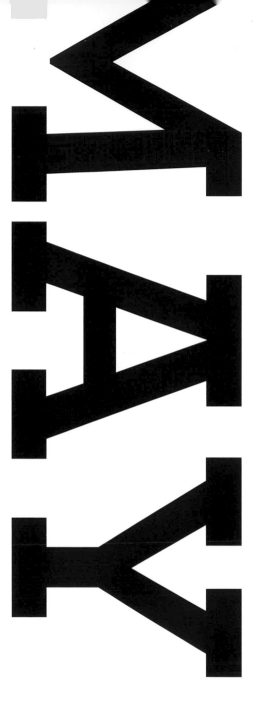

MAY IS THE Month of Flowers. The white wood anemone shyly spreads across the forest floor and the lily of the valley (voted Sweden's most popular flower) shelters near sun-warmed rocks. Mirroring the voters' love for nature, all six major political parties (save one) have flowers as emblems. Technically, the Greens' dandelion is a weed. The Social Democrats long ago branded the First of May as their own. Their polite demonstrations troop the streets and speeches echo across squares.

For an overtly secular country, Sweden's calendar is wildly religious. May begins with Ascension Day, which jokesters call Fly Away Jesus Day (*Kristiflygare*). Nine of 13 public holidays are religious. Keeping holidays — the more obscure the better — is a link to the physical past that the future will need. Sweden has been Christian since the 12th century, although travelling monks from the British Isles had been proselytizing earlier.

Just less than three quarters of the population still formally belong to the Swedish Lutheran Church. Until 2000, the Church was part of the state administration and was a repository of census data. Churches are admired mostly from the outside until Christmas rolls around. Religious gender roles are changing: 25 percent of Lutheran priests and most theology students are women.

Despite Sweden's secular style, church weddings are popular, and the prime time for nuptials is Pentecost or Whitsun week. On the seventh Sunday after Easter, the Holy Spirit descended from heaven to inspire the apostles and, apparently, weddings in Sweden. The ceremonies are scheduled to suit ever-extending families, but principally to catch the best weather.

Name changes are common, at one stage even officially encouraged. Until the mid-1800s, family surnames were mostly for the middle and upper classes while the peasants named their sons and daughters 'Gunnar, son of Sven' or Gunnar Svensson. Girls? 'Anna, son of Sven' — we're talking pre-gender-equality. Statisticians, an

Delightful May: cherry blossoms surround an old farmhouse in the ubiquitous copper-based *faluröd* paint that effectively preserves thousands of centuries-old rural buildings up and down the land. Writer August Strindberg wanted the Swedish flag to be red and green, symbolising the red houses and green fields and trees.

At the end of the 19th century, prosperous Swedish towns replaced the wooden buildings that recalled a poorer past. City centres acquired acres of stone residences, most of which still stand.

(Overleaf) The island of Ven, anchored between Sweden and Denmark, with the coast of Skåne, Sweden's southernmost province, in the background. Astronomer Tycho Brahe lived here in the late 16th century. His calculations formed the basis of Kepler's Laws, describing the way planets orbit our Sun.

influential group, complained that there were too many Svenssons and Anderssons to cope with. The rural middle classes took names from the nature around them, cutting and pasting: birch, rock, stream, branch, lake, bear, twig, island, falcon, etc. Occasionally, the mix will be an oxymoron: Mountainbeach, Seamountain or Firleaf. Johansson is the most common name, although Swedes refer to themselves as 'Svenssons' and Svensson is apparently the name most commonly used by couples booking hotel rooms for illicit love.

If you've been shopping around for a new home, chances are you bought it last month, in April, the spring peak of the housing market. Realtors like to wait for the most flattering light. Real estate purchases are fast and furious, so by May you're probably ready to visit IKEA. The ubiquitous IKEA. A biblically huge print run for its catalogue, a major exporter of Swedish food to feed its restaurants, etc. IKEA has a central roost in the nation's psyche. It's a global success sprung from the callouses of a plain-spoken country guy. It's a simple story and a source of pride. But people resent IKEA's domination of the national design aesthetic. And to rub salt in that resentment, we all use it.

This is the time of year when people rediscover the joy of sitting outdoors with a cookie and a glass of classic fruit squash. The pleasure is so seductive that a Japanese marathon runner, suffering heat exhaustion, once broke off a race to join a Stockholm family relaxing under a tree in their garden. That was during the 1912 Olympic marathon. Ashamed to rejoin his team, Shizo Kanaguri slunk back to Japan on the Trans-Siberian Railway. He returned to Stockholm in 1966 to finish the distance. These days, the Stockholm marathon is run in late May or early June.

Free access to
education from
grade school
through university
is one of the pillars
of Swedish welfare.
Children start at
age 7, and at
15 have a choice
of continuing to
senior high for
three or four years.
Graduation is
summer's happiest
day for the nation's
school-leavers.
Many of them
will continue to
study at universities
and colleges.

(Overleaf) The
quiet glory of the
Swedish coastline
in early summer: the
thousand islands
and bays of the
Tjust archipelago on
the southeast coast.

JUNI

STRAY BY A high school in the first week of June and you might stumble across boisterous crowds of parents brandishing placards. Some show infants in embarrassing potty incidents. Parked bumper-to-bumper are decorated construction vehicles, cerise Cadillacs, rickshaws and flatbed trucks. Girls in white dresses and boys in suits and ties are swept up and driven away, singing, yelling and whistling. All are wearing peaked white caps. It's high-school graduation day, commemorating a time when pupil evaluation went down to the wire. At the final oral exam, your future career and social standing were on the line. If you made it, you got the white cap and a front door exit. About 60 percent of Swedish school pupils go on to higher education.

National Day falls on June 6th. It's been a holiday only since 2005. Everyone loves free days, several of which show up in the spring and early summer: Easter, Mayday, Ascension Day, Pentecost, National Day, Midsummer Day. Salaried employees try to accumulate enough days-owing to stretch weekends with "squeeze days" when a holiday falls on Tuesday or Thursday. June 6 used to be known as Swedish Flag Day. On 16 days of the year, including UN Day and Nobel Day, everyone is encouraged to fly the banner. Few rules apply and the flag is respected indiscriminately by right and left.

Midsummer is the acme of Swedish contentment. Boats bounce across bays and inlets, or thread among islands along lacy coasts. Tipsy revellers, heads garlanded with flowers, tumble off jetties. Everything, moving or stationary, gets decorated with birch twigs and blue and yellow ribbons. Then there's the atavistic tradition of ... er, erecting the maypole as rings of dancers sing. Poets are remembered and recipes dusted off. Hormones hum.

Newspaper headlines advertise the weather weeks in advance. And on the day, children discover the ancient challenge of dancing like little frogs around the maypole. The evening brings the secular, shared euphoria of the *smörgåsbord*. One too many snaps is drunk. And so are some of us. Pickled, too, are the herring. But for the girl

Early morning on southern Gotland island. The sparse beauty of the flat, gravelly island reveals little of its history as a Hanseatic League trading centre in the 14th century. Gotland and its special dialect are beloved by holidaying mainlanders.

(Overleaf) Stockholm's Old Town, with the brackish water of the Baltic in the foreground and the fresh water of Lake Mälaren to the top. In Mediaeval times, farmers from the lake region would come here to transfer their produce to ships departing for the Baltic coasts.

or boy who sleeps this night with seven plucked wildflowers under a pillow, true love is nigh. Might we suggest yarrow, white clover, dwarf cornels, solomon's seals, lilies-of-the-valley, bluebells and of course forget-me-nots?

Early June brings the anxious wait for a potato harvest prognosis. Did winter drought or spring rains spoil the crop? TV news covers the harvest preview just to marvel at the price. The mundane spud becomes a celebrity, then gets served boiled with a knob of butter and a sprinkling of chopped parsley, on a plate with pan-fried Baltic herring.

Legend has it that a sign on a cobbler's door read: "Closed between birdcherry and lilac". According to the cobbler and consensus, the best time of the year is the week between the blooming of the bird-cherry (*Prunus padus*) and the lilac (*Syringa vulgaris*). It is, however, established that cobbler apprentices were given time off to go hiking and shake off the winter dust.

Once-destitute
fishing villages
along the Swedish
coast (here, Orust
Island) explode
into life when
vacation season
starts. A shift in
the economy away
from manufacturing
to services and
high tech has not
greatly affected
the traditional July
shutdown.

(Overleaf) No finer
summer thrill exists
for Swedes than
dancing on a jetty
to an accordion-
based band! The
waltz and jitterbug
are favoured, but
older dancers
might be able to do
the hambo, polka,
mazurka or polska,
as here at Brännö
on the west coast.

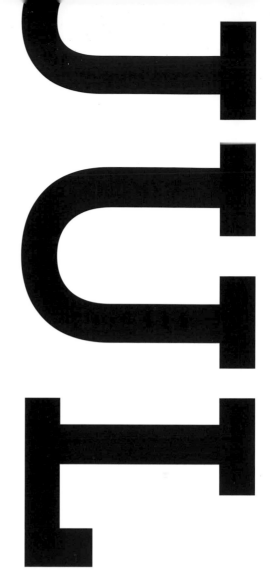

SHORT SLEEVES, BARE midriffs, ice cream, fishing in a country lake. Mmm, must be July. To counterbalance a life of functioning infrastructure and technological modernity, people are nostalgic for the primitive, rural life. Five weeks' vacation is the minimum. Every fourth employee works less than 40 hours a week, although there is a growing army of young 'no-clock' workers — mostly in IT — in an increasingly skills-based economy. Women's wages are 86 percent of men's in the private sector, 84 percent on the public side.

On a hot July Sunday afternoon, you can walk the streets and hear only the singing of birds. Manufacturing, enterprises and organisations take a break, earned or not.

Meanwhile, the countryside is humming with activity. Often literally — music festivals and performances waft tunes to the winds. The Hultsfred Festival, a rock 'n' tent happening, draws big-name acts. The Lake Siljan folk music week is famous for innovative sounds and soft kisses in moonlit parks. Stockholm has its jazz and blues week on a harbour island. Choir week on harsh Fårö Island. Arvika for electronica week.

Every tenth Swede has played a musical instrument in the last seven days. Four percent have sung in choirs in the last month. People swoon at the sound of an accordion if there are waves and seagulls in the background. The accordion and much music came from the south through Germany. The neighbouring Norwegians, behind a mountain range sometimes called *Kölen*, the keel, interacted with the fiddles of the Scottish isles instead.

It's a good month for bargains, with more than 2,000 flea markets in country seats and city suburbs.

Parliament is closed, but on the first week in July representatives of all the major political parties can be heard speechifying in the same park. Almedalen Park is in Visby, the mediaeval capital of Gotland, Sweden's island province. The island's flat, open roads bring families while Visby's lively bars draw party-makers.

For an efficient, modern society, primitive summer living can be seductive. The island of Öland off Sweden's east coast is cherished for its simplicity. *Stora Alvaret* (the Great Heath) is an expanse of low growth, moss, wild flowers and stone walls. The barrier around the pump protects it from grazing animals. This is one of Sweden's 15 sites on the UNESCO World Heritage List, areas of universal value considered essential for mankind.

(Overleaf) Själsjö fishing village on Gotland Island in the Baltic. Summer storms can be fiercer than winter ones since warmer water is more fluid.

Reindeer migrate
each year using
constant routes
and landmarks,
especially river
crossings. Reindeer
farming is the
exclusive right of
the indigenous Sami
people. The flocks
are shepherded
minimally, nowadays
using horses or
motorcycles and
satellite tracking.
Reindeer are
farmed across a
third of Sweden's
land area. Their
natural enemies are
the lynx, wolverine,
bear and wolf. And
humans — dried or
cured reindeer meat
is a delicacy.

(Overleaf) The
southern plains of
Skåne province are
the country's most
arable. When grains
are harvested late in
August, the residual
hay lies in the fields
waiting to be baled
for winter fodder.

THE MOON IS bloated but nights are now dark. Some warmth remains and in fortunate years, one evening will be chosen for spreading outdoor trestle tables with paper tablecloths, getting out the paper lanterns and plotting the crayfish party! Here, hearty indulgence in hard liquor is actually encouraged.

The *kräftor* (freshwater crustaceans, crayfish, mudbug, crawdad) are boiled, steeped in dill and brine, then sucked, shelled and devoured. Flimsy paper hats are put on and ditties are sung. The short, pithy drinking songs, unique to Sweden and Swedish-speaking Finland, are the nation's living poetry: every year new songs crop up to be remembered and repeated at next year's parties. The song canon tends to the farcical. And what a joy it is to witness one's normally reserved acquaintances, now giggling and tipsy, shouting risqué doggerel.

Drinking habits at crayfish parties mirror the nation's: a few people get plastered but most drink at a tacitly agreed pace. Aficionados take as much care as winemakers, flavouring grain or potato vodka with herbs and spices such as horseradish or roasted fennel seeds. Or forest fruits like rosehip, lingonberries and blueberries.

The third Thursday in August is the unofficial opening of the fermented herring season. This is Baltic herring soaked in lactic acid and packed in cans that literally bulge with odorous gases (hydrogen sulphide, butyric acid, etc.). Some airlines won't let you carry the tins on board because of the pressurisation issue. (They don't actually explode.) Because the Baltic Sea is brackish, not saline, northern Sweden used to lack easy access to salt. Innovation was needed to preserve food. Pickling, curing and drying are still widely used. Thin filets of innocent-seeming but pungent fish are spread on prime hard bread with chopped raw onion and boiled almond potato as company. Purists drink milk.

On 10 August 1628, the pride of the Swedish navy, the warship *Vasa*, sank in Stockholm's harbour. She was on her maiden voyage, overloaded with cannon and 500 sculptures, including 60 of lions.

Turning Torso, Malmö's eye-catching landmark, was designed by Spanish architect Santiago Calatrava from one of his sculptures. It consists of nine segments of five-storey pentagons and was the tallest residential building in the EU when completed in 2005.

(Overleaf) The Skuleskogen national park has no roads over its 3,062 hectares, only hiking tracks. This is one of 29 protected areas. Sweden was the first country in Europe to have national parks.

Sweden's most popular museum is dedicated to a disaster: the embarrassing sinking of the over-decorated, top-heavy regal warship *Vasa* in 1628, only a few hundred metres from the shipyard in Stockholm harbour.

The royal palace at Drottningholm, a leafy island near Stockholm. The palace is on the UNESCO World Heritage List.

(Overleaf) The snowy southern peak (centre-right) of Kebnekaise is officially Sweden's highest point but it consists partly of ice, melting as the climate warms. The northern ridge (closer in this photo) will ultimately assume the title.

King Gustavus Adolphus had ordered extra cannon, making the ship unstable. At the seaworthiness trial, crewmen ran from one side of the ship to the other, but the test was called off because the ship was pitching violently. Who would tell the King? Apparently no one, because the ship went down a few hundred metres from its launching place. Shock or embarrassment erased the memory of the shipwreck site until a lone researcher found it 333 years later. The world's only surviving 17th-century ship rests inside a world-class museum in Stockholm with 15 million visitors at last count.

At the end of August or the beginning of September, the annual measurement is made of Sweden's highest mountain, Kebnekaise. Because the peak of the currently 2,100 metre-high mountain is glacier, global warming is whittling it down — it is currently 21 metres lower than when first measured. Kebnekaise is the jewel of the Swedish mountain world.

By the last week of August, schools again fill with the eager, the reluctant and all their friends. A new academic year has begun.

A milk cow in the woods — currently a rare sight. In 1930, there were four times as many cows, and now they're mostly kept indoors on a regulated diet. No anthill lunches.

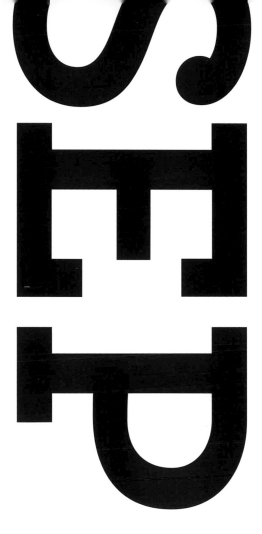

"PROUD SPRING ARISES; the weak call it autumn." Turn-of-the-20th-century poet Erik Axel Karlfeldt was oiling his hiking boots when he wrote that. Autumn is when the Swedish brain clicks into warpspeed: ideas are born, books are opened, DIY seriously considered, evening classes thirsting for discoveries launch. A brief mourning period for the brief summer ends abruptly.

The woods are full of blueberries/bilberries, cloudberries and the prince of them all, the lingonberry or cowberry. It is a little cousin of the cranberry family, used as a savoury preserve. Try it with pan-fried Baltic herring.

Like their cranberry cousins, lingonberries are harvested in the forest with small rakes. Wily entrepreneurs fly in teams of pickers from as far off as Thailand and China.

The benzoic acid in the berry is a natural preservative, and lingon is time-honoured as a summer berry easily kept for winter use. Widespread poverty prompted Swedish ingenuity to use pickling, drying, curing, smoking and fermenting to store food. A common modern trick is to marinate raw salmon, gravlax.

(Gravlax recipe. Buy a chunk of filet. Extract any bones with tweezers. Rub with equal units of sugar and salt and half a unit of chopped dill. Plastic-bag it in your fridge, turning occasionally, for 2–3 days. Scrape off marinade. Skin, cut into cutlets and garnish with fresh dill. Lemon boats alongside.)

September is wild mushroom season. Hunting and picking them is a national infatuation. The fungi have wondrous names: Parasol mushroom, Horn of Plenty, Shaggy ink cap, Saffron milk cap, Woolly milk cap. Dinner favourites are the Cep, the Morel and the Chanterelle. Watch out for the deadly Fly agaric and the instructively named Death cap.

Mushroomers say their hikes through dripping forests, mud underfoot, are escapades into nature. When the sun sets they come back beaming.

The legs of Poseidon, kept hydrated by a fountain in central Gothenburg. The Swedish-American sculptor Carl Milles had a liking for mythical themes. His works were commissioned for several Swedish cities as well as Rockefeller Center in New York.

(Overleaf) Sweden's second city, Gothenburg. Founded in 1621 by the Reformation era empire-builder, King Gustavus Adolphus, the city remains Sweden's gateway to the west and the largest port in the Nordic area. Thanks to the flow of warm Gulf Stream waters, autumn in Gothenburg is generally mild for its high latitude.

On a farm in Kall, Jämtland province, hay is dried on racks, the old-fashioned way.

It's the beginning of the apple and pear harvest. Swedes accept as gospel that Swedish apples are superior to those of any other geography. It's a good argument, considering the delicate Transparant Blanche, the crisp Åkerö and the fragrant Aroma.

Every fourth year in September, voters can choose national candidates for the single-chamber Riksdag as well as regional and local government. Parties need 4 percent of the popular vote for Riksdag representation. Voting is proportional, so policy often takes precedence over individuals' profiles. Election campaigns are brief. The most conspicuous sign is the (detachable) posters on city lampposts and handrails. On the day, about 80 percent of eligible voters stuff their three envelopes with the coloured lists available from officials or, as you approach the polling station, from volunteers or even political celebrities. Respect for politics and politicians shifts, but single-issue or malcontent parties have difficulty surviving. Just under half of all parliamentarians are women.

In the south, the deciduous trees are turning yellow and red. But 80 percent of Sweden's trees are spruce (*Picea*) with needle-like evergreen foliage. Well over half the country is covered by forest. The tallest tree is the pine. Sweden's greatest natural resource (alongside iron ore) came from Asia before the Ice Age. The great forestry barons, entering banquet halls on horseback, are no more, but paper is still a mainstay industry. Way back, woodcutters used to slash pines a year before felling. This induced the tree to produce extra resinous sap to heal the wound, giving durable timber.

September is a month of several seasons. Summer lingers on the plains and littorals of the southern provinces, but it's autumn for most of the rest and already winter in the highlands of Lapland. Temperatures diverge by as much as 40 degrees Celsius. In Europe only Russia has such a latitude span. Birds are taking off literally and figuratively for the south. At least 90 percent leave, the arctic tern taking three months for its trip all the way to the Southern Ocean. It'll be back.

October can bring
four seasons
at once, with
balmy days in the
extreme south and
snowstorms in the
far north. On calm
days, it is beautiful
everywhere. The
melancholy of
a lost summer
meets autumn at
Akkafjället.

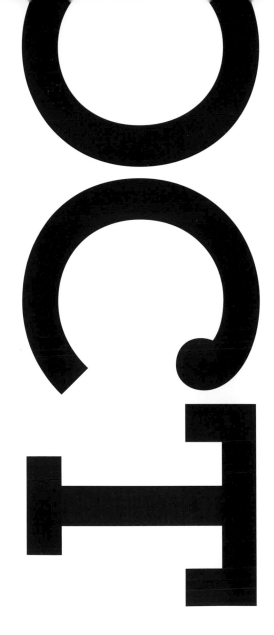

TIME TO HIDE for the king of the forest, the moose (*Alces alces*). The moose hunt may technically have started on the first of September in the north, but October is when most of the rest of the country loads up. (The season is staggered to allow calves to grow.) Yellowing leaves still provide cover for the antlered majesty but he'll need it every day — from an hour before sunrise until sundown — to the end of February. Hunters wear garish orange hatbands to alert other hunters and fool their colour-blind prey. A sprig of spruce in the hatband signals a bagged moose. Hunting season coincides with mating season. For an attractive scent, bulls kick up a pile of moss and twigs, urinate on it, then roll in it. What moose cow could resist?

When clear-cutting was the forestry industrial standard in the 1970s and '80s, weeds flourished in the open spaces: breakfast, lunch and dinner for a moose population that fattened and multiplied. Moose sightings were common. With clear-cutting now less common, the population has declined. About 100,000 moose bite the forest moss every year to wind up in savoury stews.

Eighteenth-century naturalist Carl Linnaeus invented the system of classifying plants and animals and named the moose *Alces alces*. North America has four species and Asia two.

Schools break for a week at the end October to give children relaxation and, ideally, exercise. Only in the north will there be enough snow for snowball fights. But winter sports are starting up. The most traditional team sport is bandy, although it attracts barely a tenth of the crowds that see ice hockey. A Scottish game called shinny evolved into ice hockey and bandy, which is played on ice with curved sticks and a small orange ball that TV doesn't scan well. Pink and fluorescent balls have been trialled but there's something sweet about the small orange. Newcomers to Sweden, standing outdoors in below-zero temperatures, get an acoustic surprise when a goal is scored: the smattering sound of gloved hands applauding.

The king. The solitary bull moose surveys his domain. His nine-tined antlers indicate a powerful beast. The annual moose hunt starts in mid-September in the far north, but most regions begin in October.

Late October is when the Nobel Prizes are made public. The prize with greatest celebrity factor is the peace award. Because Sweden and Norway were in a union when Alfred Nobel wrote his will in 1895, he stipulated that the 'brother nation' have that honour. Sweden got all the others: Medicine, Physics, Chemistry and Literature, which attracts the most public speculation. As soon as the committee at the Swedish Academy decides whose canon best represents a compromise between modern excellence and what Alfred Nobel actually wanted — idealistic writing — a press conference is called. Then, at precisely one p.m., an ornate timepiece chimes the hour and the Academy's permanent secretary emerges to announce the world's most prestigious prize for writing. The Swedish Academy, its historic sapling planted by the culture-loving despot Gustav III (1746–1792), is a factory of thought and dedication, appreciated as a world treasury of writing.

Where other countries excel in wrapped candy bars, Swedish convenience stores proffer rainbow rows of cheap candies. Swedes prefer their sugar in caramels and toffees, nougats, jellies, fondants, marshmallows, marzipans, truffles, cotton candies and licorices, chewing gums in shapes of stars, bears, discs, blobs and ... thingies. Desserts are less fashionable than in other countries. But a cake in a café (*konditori*) is a treat few can resist. October 4 is Cinnamon Roll Day. Consumption of sugar has been constant or declining. Don't forget though, brain cells depend on a supply of glucose from the blood.

October used to be the month for moving house. Until its abolition in 1945, a system of indentured rural labour maintained a lowest class in Sweden. Hired on annual contracts and paid primarily in kind, the workers were permitted to move only in October. And move they did, from unkind bosses to potentially kinder ones. Now, it's mostly younger people who move about. After they've passed 30, most people move only within their town or region. A majority now lives in urban areas, and generally in apartments. Municipal non-profit housing has been shrinking — not in size of apartments, which are larger than in most European countries — but in number. Governments have preferred to get people off their support lists and into home ownership. Slums are non-existent although many areas are ethnically or economically unbalanced and some are drab. Influential local government bodies such as Stockholm's 'Beauty Council' have kept cities largely homogeneous if not striking.

Urban legend has it that the Stockholm branch of the swanky NK department store (facing page) has so many lights that it needs no central heating. False, but almost believable when autumn shoppers swarm.

The daily fish auctions in Gothenburg. The product is so fresh and the crushed ice so generous and effective that there's scarcely a whiff of fish.

Visiting foodies quickly find the Östermalm Saluhall in the centre of Stockholm with its richness of game, fish, fresh produce and restaurants.

(Overleaf) Rapadalen valley, Sarek National Park, in the moonlight. Nowhere else in Europe is there such an expanse of wilderness. The valley is the artery of Sarek.

The cruellest month. All hope of warmth is gone and the transforming snow has not yet arrived unless you're in the far north. Weekends are for DVDs and hot chocolate until you realise that the only way to survive the looming winter is to get out and face it. Dress warm.

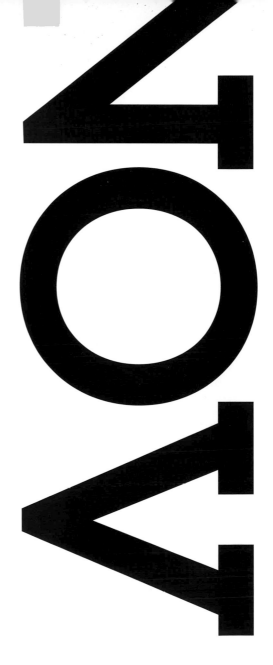

IT'S OVERCAST. A wet mist slides down over you. Buses are sprayed with dirty, crusty snow. And yet many are happy at the onset of winter. There's less guilt for staying indoors, and all that magical snow to look forward to, softening edges in the country and reflecting street light in cities. November is when people get serious about Sunday walks. Kids skid around on the artificial ice in the parks. Sawdusted paths through suburban woods are gridlocked. Please keep to the right.

Winter is when it is legitimate to be melancholy. The culture accommodates gloom. Come spring, people will shrug off that dark woollen cape and embrace joy.

All Souls' Day, another of the many religious holidays, is for lighting candles in cemeteries. Newspaper obituary notices often include a verse and an illustration indicating the deceased's main hobby: cats, fishing, classic cars, etc. A matter-of-fact, science-loving people, Swedes are not normally bothered with the afterlife. Seventy percent are cremated at death.

Early winter is dinner-party season. Here are the rules: Arrive exactly on time. With flowers or wine. Remove shoes if it's muddy outside. (Forgot your indoor shoes? Oh-oh.) Don't drink faster than the host. Leave before midnight, by taxi or designated driver: drinking and driving is uncool. A single glass of wine will put you over the limit.

If Swedes are traditional when entertaining, they're casual and innovative at work. And they like to work in groups. Teamwork means getting people with common interests to work together. In other countries, such as the US, goals are decided in advance and teams work towards them, using conflict if necessary. Like the Japanese, Swedes like to see how far they can get by agreeing. One of the major labour market achievements of the last century was an implicit pact between unions and employers to get along without surrendering their own interests.

Swedes like to think of themselves as a compassionate people

With daylight dwindling, cities begin to look enchanting. A row of identical office buildings in downtown Stockholm represents the fascination with power and optimism that characterised 1960s architecture. These buildings were once considered ugly, but are now classic.

114

with a durable engagement in world affairs and a tolerance towards immigrants. Yes, there have been attacks on mosque construction projects and yes, it's demonstrably hard for people with unfamiliar-sounding names to get jobs they're qualified for. But Sweden is also consistently good at foreign aid, up there with the Netherlands and Norway. An islamophobic party, the Sweden Democrats, now has a firm toehold in the Riksdag. The anti-immigration virus has infected this country too. But tolerance lives: Sweden has received more applications from Iraqi refugees than any other European country. The small city of Södertälje, close to Stockholm, has taken in more refugees from the Iraq conflict than the US and Canada combined. Södertälje is also home to the largest group of Assyrians in Europe.

Protected by mountains and seas, Sweden was homogeneous until the 20th century. The 21st is a new story.

Will the coming winter be another fertile one for the calicivirus, producing a form of gastroenteritis descriptively called 'winter vomiting sickness'? Let's hope not.

In the foreground, ferries that ply the Stockholm archipelago for most of the year hunker down for the icy winter. Behind them, the three-masted schooner *af Chapman*, now a tourist hostel permanently at anchor, offers warm bunks and zero risk of rough seas.

BY NOW IT'S getting hard to share a seat on buses — the plump down jackets people use to keep out the cold increase personal volume considerably. The front corridor at the daycare centre is a mountain of children's jump suits, and getting kids clothed and unclothed is an interminable operation. Christmas trees have been up in town squares for two weeks.

The Nobel ceremonies are held in Stockholm on the 10th. The daytime presentation from the hands of the monarch is followed by a gala banquet in the ornate City Hall. A live broadcast blends gossip and erudition, with comments on dresses and celebrity cleavage intermixed with pithy explanations of achievements in physics, medicine and economics. Alfred Nobel himself would enjoy the evening; he liked the good life in Paris and San Remo and the company of attractive women. But, painfully shy, he needed a topic of conversation and peace was his favourite. The City of San Remo, Italy, where Nobel spent his last years and where he died on 10 December 1896, sends truckloads of flowers each year for the ceremonies.

December is party time, often centred on the sticky, sweet mulled wine known as *glögg* and ginger biscuits. *Glögg* combines red wine, spirits and spices, taken in tiny glasses or cups into which you spoon raisins and blanched almonds. A little goes a long way. Glitter is optional, but ambitious hosts decorate the doorstep with fir branches.

December is also a month of lights, electric or otherwise. High-rise office windows display electric versions of the Advent candles. Big paper stars like Japanese lanterns hang in apartment windows. Private parties signal their location with thick candles in tins outside entrances. Light therapy challenges the demon darkness. The first word Swedish children learn is often *lampa* (lamp or light).

St. Lucia Day on the 13th replaces an ancient celebration of the winter solstice, when barnyard animals were said to be able to talk to each other and the long winter was halved. St. Lucia was believed

The festival of St. Lucia, originally honouring a Sicilian saint, now has more connection with ancient winter solstice rites. In the old days, it was said that barnyard animals could talk on this day. Today, the voices come from children's choirs.

(Overleaf) Royalty and dignitaries listen respectfully as one of the world's most talented scientists, economists, authors, or doctors delivers the Nobel Address on the evening after the prize ceremony. The venue is the Blue Hall in Stockholm's City Hall. It's not blue because the architect changed his mind.

to have lived in Sicily. Some say that when a saint saved Lucia's sick mother from death, Lucia abandoned marriage plans and gave her dowry to the poor. Her fiancé took her to court and she was sentenced to a brothel but a thousand men, using oxen, could not drag her in. The modern custom involves angelic girl children dressed in white, although there is a role for Staffan the Stable boy, the comic relief. The white-robed children sing while lights dim and candles flicker. The custom came from nostalgic Swedish colonies in America a century ago and originally mandated a crown of lit candles in a blonde little sweetheart's hair, predictably risk-filled in a milling crowd of excited kids.

Winter solstice on the 21st is when the country breathes a deep sigh of relief: finally, we can at least imagine light at the end of the tunnel! In Stockholm, office commuters might miss sun-up at about 8:30 am and certainly miss sundown at around 2:45 pm. They're still lucky — up above the polar circle in the city of Kiruna, for example, it's pitch black for about three weeks in mid-winter. Sweden is in the west-wind belt with chiefly southwesterly or westerly winds. The frigid winds of the Russian steppes seldom intrude.

Christmas and most other important holidays are celebrated on the eve. Christmas Day is for relaxing, except for whoever is preparing the *smörgåsbord*. The dishes are based on simple country fare — a way of gourmandizing while remaining down-to-earth. Staples include ham, pickled herring, jellied veal, boiled ling, beetroot and herring salad, and the essential meatballs, all washed down with snaps and sweet Christmas beer or a mixture of stout, port and lemonade. Then finish up with rice porridge. Phew!

Does bathwater run down the drain counterclockwise in the northern hemisphere and clockwise in the south? Fact: reindeer corralled in December will always run counterclockwise. Reindeer are also the only deer species where both males and females have horns. (Insert your own joke here about gender equality in Sweden.)

Come quarter to midnight on New Year's Eve, the nation's current favourite actor will be found breathing mist into the cold night air at Stockholm's Skansen outdoor museum, a folklore heirloom. As television lights flare, with the background a sky of pyrotechnical colour, the actor clears his throat. Then, as every year since the 1920s, the actor reads a poem written by the Englishman, Alfred Tennyson: "Ring out the old, ring in the new / Ring, happy bells, across the snow / The year is going, let him go / Ring out the false, ring in the true." And ring in longer days.

This time of year used to be harsh on the island of Bullerö in the Stockholm archipelago, but Christmas brought festivity and an occasion to eat the best dried or cured food saved from the summer.

Christmas time, with the Old Town in the foreground and the Grand Hôtel across the water. From the quay in front of the hotel, ferries traffic the archipelago.

(Overleaf) The brick cliffs of Söder, Stockholm's south island. Once the poorest district, Söder is today both tough and trendy.

Facts about Sweden

Area: 174,000 sq mi (450,000 sq km), the third largest country in Western Europe
Forests: 53%
Mountains: 11%
Cultivated land: 8%
Lakes and rivers: 9%
Longest north-south distance: 978 mi (1,574 km)
Longest east-west distance: 310 mi (499 km)
Capital: Stockholm
Population: 9.9 million inhabitants
Languages: Swedish; recognised minority languages: Sami (Lapp), Finnish, Meänkieli (Tornedalen Finnish), Yiddish, Romani Chib
Form of government: Constitutional monarchy, parliamentary democracy
Parliament: The *Riksdag*, with 349 members in one chamber
Religion: In practice, Sweden is very secularised. The Church of Sweden is Evangelical Lutheran; co-exists with many other beliefs
Life expectancy: men 79 years, women 83 years

Average temperatures

	January	July
Malmö	31.6°F (-0.2°C)	62.2°F (+16.8°C)
Stockholm	27.0°F (-2.8°C)	63.0°F (+17.2°C)
Kiruna	3.2°F (-16.0°C)	55.0°F (+12.8°C)

Daylight

	January 1	July 1
Malmö	7 hours	17 hours
Stockholm	6 hours	18 hours
Kiruna	0 hours	24 hours

Stockholmers, like all Swedes, like to light up the winter. Candlelight dinners are frequent; electric lights are put in windows for the delight of passers-by, and any excuse for fireworks is a good one.

Geography

With 9.7 million inhabitants, Sweden is a small nation – smaller than Belgium and only half the size of the Netherlands. But in terms of surface area, Sweden is a big country – the third largest in Western Europe – almost the same size as Spain and France and bigger than California. If you could rotate Sweden like the hand of a clock 180 degrees, with the southern tip of the country at the base of the hand, then the northern tip would wind up on the same latitude as Naples in southern Italy. Sweden's coastline is over 2,700 kilometers (or almost 1,700 miles) long – a distance equivalent to that between Montreal and Miami on the east coast of North America. The large surface area and limited number of inhabitants make Sweden a sparsely populated country. Almost 90 percent of the population lives in the southern half of the country.

Nature

Because Sweden is a long country that stretches from north to south, the contrasts between the various parts of the country are dramatic. Far up north are the mighty Lapland fells, with their bald mountains, ice-blue glaciers and remote swamplands. The vast majority of land in northern and central Sweden is covered in dense coniferous forests, interspersed with thousands of lakes and rushing rivers that run from the mountains in the west toward the Baltic Sea in the east. Along the extensive coastline are a large number of unique archipelagos, made up of tens of thousands of islands and rocks of various sizes, most of them uninhabited. Farthest south lies the province of Skåne, with the most fertile farmland in Sweden, complete with undulating fields, lush deciduous forests and rolling hills.

Climate

Sweden's northern location gives the country a cold climate which is tempered, however, by the warm Gulf Stream running through the northern Atlantic Ocean. It is the Gulf Stream that makes it possible for people to live in Sweden. Areas at similar latitudes, like Canada, Alaska and Siberia, consist largely of barren, uninhabited land. The changes in the seasons are dramatic: a warm, light and pleasant summer, a colorful autumn and a long, dark winter followed by a bright, refreshing and vivid spring. It is these changes in light that are so characteristic of Sweden and also give rise to the phenomenon of the midnight sun, when the sun shines in the northern parts of the country around the clock during the summer. The counterpart to this is the intense darkness of winter, which is only broken by a few short hours of daylight, and by the famous northern lights, which dance across the Arctic sky during the winter months.

People

Over the last fifty years, the population of Sweden has experienced a dramatic transformation, as hundreds of thousands of people from different parts of the world have immigrated. A large percentage of the inhabitants in Sweden today have a foreign background. The largest groups of immigrants come from the other Nordic countries, from the former Yugoslavia, from Iraq, Iran and Africa. Many of these immigrants came to Sweden as refugees in the past twenty years. Immigration has also meant a dramatic change over a short period of time and transformed Sweden into a multicultural, international country. Roughly one hundred years ago, when Sweden was still a country of poor peasants, it was, in contrast, a nation of emigrants. From the end of the 19th century to 1930, no fewer than 1.5 million Swedes – a fourth of the population – emigrated, with most going to North America.

History

Sweden's ancient history is violent and dramatic, filled with war and conquests. It began with the Viking plunderings in about the 11th century and continued as time went by with the endless military campaigns under warrior kings like Gustav II Adolf and Karl XII. In the 17th century, Sweden was a great power in Europe, its territories stretching over large parts of the Baltic Sea region. By the 18th century, Sweden had become so impoverished by all its fighting that peace had to be achieved if the country was to survive. Sweden has lived in peace since 1814, which has been one of the most important factors in the development and well-being of the country. Sweden was one of the few European countries not involved in the two world wars of the 20th century. In the post-war period, Sweden has been renowned for its role in working for international peace.

Development

As late as the end of the 19th century, Sweden was one of the poorest countries in Europe. Record economic development began only when the railroads were built and allowed access to the enormous assets of forests, iron ore and hydropower in northern Sweden. In just fifty years, Sweden was transformed into one of the richest countries in the world. Most of the country's major international export companies were founded during this period, many of them on the basis of a large number of ingenious inventions – the ball bearing, the milk separator, the unmanned lighthouse, dynamite, the ship propeller, the steam turbine and the refrigerator, just to name a few. In more modern times, the Swedish tradition of inventions has continued with the development of such innovations as the pacemaker, the AXE telephone exchange, the computer mouse, GPS for navigation and Bluetooth for Internet mobility.

Trade

Even today, Swedish basic industry, steel and paper production, accounts for more than one fifth of the country's export income. But by far the largest share of exports, about 60 percent, consists of what falls under the broader category of mechanical engineering industries, which includes the automotive, electrical, chemical and telecom industries. Swedish industry is research-intensive and is characterized by a high level of technological development. IT, biotechnology and environmental technology are often mentioned as some of the most important Swedish future-oriented industries, but what have come to be called "creative industries," such as design, fashion and music, are also considered important for the future. Given the size of its population, Sweden has had a surprisingly large number of multinational export companies and brands – AstraZeneca, ABB, IKEA, Ericsson, Electrolux, H&M and Absolut, to name a few.

Nobel

The Nobel Prize was established at the end of the 19th century under the will of Alfred Nobel, one of Sweden's many great inventors and industrialists of the era and, among other things, the inventor of dynamite. The Nobel Prizes quickly became recognised as the world's most prestigious civic awards. The Nobel Prize is awarded by the Swedish monarch in four categories – literature, medicine, physics and chemistry (since 1968, Sweden's central bank the *Riksbank*, has sponsored the Alfred Nobel Memorial Prize in Economics) – in an annual ceremony in Stockholm on Nobel Day, December 10. The fifth original Nobel Prize, the Peace Prize, is awarded the same day in the Norwegian capital, Oslo, the location being explained by the fact that Norway and Sweden were politically unified when Nobel was alive.

Society

The prosperity that accumulated with Sweden's economic advancement in the 20th century was distributed among the population in a way that was unique in the Western world. High taxes paid for a large public sector and financed what are known as general welfare systems, including publicly financed healthcare, childcare, schools, senior care and many other systems to provide security. The principle was, and remains, that every citizen, regardless of background, income or other conditions, would be guaranteed basic security in every phase of life. This is "the Swedish welfare policy," based on a market economy with strong elements of redistributive policy, which came to be known internationally as "the third way," various aspects of which have served as an example in many other countries.

Equality

Even though Sweden is far from being a society where everyone is equal, the belief that everyone is of equal worth and has the same rights has prevailed in the development of the modern Swedish welfare state. Compared internationally, Sweden has come a long way in its efforts to guarantee the rights of once vulnerable groups such as women, children ... Swedish laws and customs include a system of rules and regulations that prohibit discrimination against people on the basis of gender, ethnic origin, physical, mental or intellectual disabilities, sexual orientation and political and religious conviction.

Form of government

Universal suffrage for men and women was introduced in Sweden in 1919. Sweden has a one-chamber parliament, the *Riksdag*, with 349 members elected from all parts of the country. The Swedish parliament is one of the world's most gender-equitable. Almost 50 percent of its members have been women during the past three four-year terms. There are currently eight parties represented in the *Riksdag*, divided into two blocs – the Alliance (the Moderate Party, Liberal Party, Center Party and Christian Democrats) on one side and the Social Democrats, Left Party and Green Party on the other. The newest political group with parliamentary representation is the immigration-critical Sweden Democrats. The dominant party since the early 20th century has been the Social Democrats, who have governed the country most of the time since the 1920s with a few brief periods out of office. There was a major change in the country's domestic and foreign policy in 1995 when Sweden became a member of the European Union (EU). In 2003, however, the Swedish people voted against giving up the Swedish krona and joining the EU's euro zone.

Education

Sweden has nine years of compulsory schooling, which begins at the age of 6 or 7. Almost every student then continues on to upper secondary education for three years, in some 20 different programs. Roughly a quarter of students then go on to study at a university or college. Higher education is also government-funded to a large extent and also features a system of student loans financed by the government. Sweden is one of the countries that invests the largest percentage of GDP in education – an important policy priority given that education is considered the most important investment in the future in a knowledge-intensive society like Sweden's. The Swedish education system has also become more international now that the

European Union is making it easier to study abroad and Swedish educational institutions have become increasingly attractive to students and teachers from around the world.

Monarchy

Sweden is a constitutional monarchy in which the king is head of state, without political power, and with only representative and ceremonial functions. The current king of Sweden, Carl XVI Gustaf, has been on the throne since 1973. His wife, Queen Silvia, grew up in Brazil and has a German father and a Brazilian mother. The successor to the throne is Crown Princess Victoria (born in 1977), the oldest of three children in the royal family and big sister of Prince Carl Philip and Princess Madeleine. In 2012, popular Victoria and her consort, Prince Daniel, delighted the nation with their first born, Princess Estelle. This future heiress to the throne saw the birth in 2014 of a cousin, Princess Leonore, daughter of Madeleine and her American husband Christopher O'Neill.

Religion

Sweden broke with the Catholic Church in the 16th century and has been a decidedly Lutheran country since then. In modern times, the importance of religion has declined and Sweden has become one of the most secular countries in the world, even though roughly 80 percent of its inhabitants formally belong to the Church of Sweden. For most Swedes, the church today provides largely ceremonial functions, such as baptisms, confirmations, graduation ceremonies, weddings and funerals. With the considerable migration to Sweden of recent decades, the country has become multicultural in a religious sense as well. After Christianity, Islam is now the second largest religion in Sweden.

Culture

Sweden has a rich selection to offer people interested in culture, whether their interest is literature, architecture, dance, contemporary fashion and design or other creative pursuits. Swedish cultural policy has been successful in spreading cultural amenities to a broad population, with a well-developed infrastructure of museums, libraries, theatres, cinemas and other cultural institutions across the country. Most of Sweden's national institutions, many of them of world renown, are in Stockholm, including the Royal Opera, the Royal Dramatic Theatre, Nationalmuseum, Moderna Museet and others. The last decade in particular has also seen an extensive internationalisation of Swedish cultural life, especially in popular culture, with Swedish artists, actors and fashion designers attracting worldwide attention in fields such as music, literature, art, design, fashion and media.

Music, design, fashion and "lifestyle"

Especially over the past decade, Sweden has experienced strong growth and attracted international attention in the field known as "commercial culture" or "popular culture" – pop music, design, fashion, architecture, gastronomy, media and advertising, etc. These industries, now known under the collective term "creative industries," are among Sweden's most important future-oriented industries. The Swedish capital, Stockholm, in particular has received a great deal of international coverage in the world press over the past few years as one of the top scenes for an urban lifestyle, fashion and trends, alongside world cities like London, Paris, Milan and New York.

Food & drink

Many of the classic Swedish specialties such as gravlax (marinated salmon) and pickled herring, are distinguished by the traditional contrast in flavours of sweet, sour and salty. These typical flavours are also found in traditional Swedish methods of preparing the delicacies that the country's forests, lakes, rivers and seas provide – game, berries, mushrooms and seafood. Over the past few decades, Swedish food traditions have embraced influences from every corner of the gastronomic world. Swedish chefs have become internationally renowned for their creativity and have triumphed in a great number of prestigious international cooking competitions. There is a large and varied selection of interesting restaurants, not just in the major cities but throughout the country, where people interested in gastronomy can enjoy quality Swedish ingredients prepared and served in the most modern and innovative of ways.

Sports

Swedes are enthusiastic about sports and fitness. Nearly every second Swede between the ages of 7 and 70 belongs to an athletic association of some type, and there is a broad range of sports and activities throughout the country available to people of every age. The biggest sports are soccer and ice hockey. For girls in particular, horseback riding and gymnastics are also sports with large, broad appeal. It is indeed this breadth of appeal that explains Sweden's remarkable success in many fields of athletics given the size of its population. The two greatest modern-day athletes in Sweden have been tennis player Björn Borg and the downhill skier Ingemar Stenmark.

Cities

The three largest cities in Sweden are Stockholm, Göteborg (Gothenburg) and Malmö. Stockholm, the capital, is the largest, with roughly 2 million inhabitants in the city and its suburbs, and is generally recognised as one of the most beautiful capital cities in the world, built on thirteen islands where Lake Mälaren flows into the Baltic Sea. Göteborg, on the west coast, is a major centre of shipping, industry and a variety of events, with some of Sweden's largest companies, such as SKF, headquartered there. Malmö, in the southernmost province of Sweden, is part of what may be northern Europe's most dynamic growth region since the city was linked to the nearby Danish capital of Copenhagen in 2000 by the impressive Öresund Link.

The text Facts about Sweden was first published by the Swedish Institute on Sweden.se, Sweden's official website.

Picture Sources

Jacket, front Hans Strand/
Briljans

Jacket, back Jeppe Wikström

Lars Bygdemark 6, 44, 50,
52–53, 76, 78–79, 92–93

Göran Ekström 33, 105

Jonas Forsberg/
Naturfotograferna 16–17

Eddie Granlund/Naturbild 112

Claes Grundsten 20–21, 36,
46–47, 82, 88–89, 117, 126

Tore Hagman 12, 23, 24, 28, 32,
49, 68, 70–71, 94, 97, 98–99, 100,
108a, 110–111

Malcolm Hanes 56–57

Sven Halling/Naturbild 15,
84–85

Ben Nilsson/
Big Ben Productions 25

Torbjörn Lilja/
Naturfotograferna 26–27

Ulf Palm/Scanpix 34–35

Magnus Rietz/Johnér 59,
74–75

Anders Ryman 54

Håkan Sandbring/Sydpol 73, 87

Jan Schützer/
Naturfotograferna 116

Hans Strand 39, 40, 63, 64–65,
66–67, 102, 107, 130–131

Erik G Svensson 108b, 109

Roger Turesson 124–125

Jeppe Wikström 4, 8–9, 11,
18, 31, 41, 42–43, 60–61, 62, 77,
80–81, 90, 91, 115, 118–119, 120,
123, 128, 129, 132